THE POWER CORD

40 DAY MARRIAGE PRAYER DEVOTIONAL AND JOURNAL

for Your Prayer Journey

by Hayward and Starlette Jean

"And if one prevail against him, two shall withstand him; and a threefold cord is not quickly broken."

ECCLESIASTES 4:12 (KJV)

SPEAK LIFE PUBLISHING

ORANGEBURG, SC

Published by: Speak Life Publishing

Cover Design and Book Layout by Greg Jackson, Thinkpen Design, Springdale, Arkansas

ISBN: 97989856055

Unless otherwise noted, Scripture quotations are taken from The King James Version of the Bible, Copyright © 1984, by Thomas Nelson.

Scripture quotations marked AMP are taken from the Amplified Bible, Copyright © 1954, 1958, 1962, 1964, 1965, 1987 by The Lockman Foundation. Used by permission. (www. lockman.org)

Library of Congress Control Number: 2022930793

Printed in the United States of America

ACKNOWLEDGEMENTS

Thank you, God, for choosing us to impact
and share the heart of Christ for marriages.
Without the Lord we would be absolutely nothing!

To our dynamic children, thank you for being amazing!
We love being your parents.

Micah Jean

Malachi Jean

Imani Jean

To the first-round editor of this project, thank you!

G. Miki Hayden

To a few dynamic couples, thank you for your support
in reviewing the final stages of this project!

Mr. and Mrs. Roland (Carlette) Foreman

Mr. and Mrs. Glover (Dorthy) Richberg

Bishop and Pastor Ed (Carleen) Riley

To the amazing designer of this book project,
thank you for advice and expertise.

Greg Jackson

To the amazing community that supports this journey of
empowering engaged and married couples, thank you!

The Power Cord Community

DEDICATION TO
POWER CORD COUPLES

We dedicate this prayer journal to couples who want to ensure their marriages are all God intends them to be.

No matter the length of time a couple has been married, prayer is vital. Our heart for marriage is that we should always strive to resemble the way Christ loved the Church and the way the Church should love Christ.

Our aim is to promote, encourage, and strengthen Kingdom of God marriages.

We hope this prayer journal brings joy, peace, understanding, and a deeper level of spiritual intimacy in marriages.

Our marriages can and will thrive as we remain connected to the Power Source, hence creating a Power Cord that is not easily broken!

Keep praying God's will for your marriage, as you live God's will for your marriage!

With Love,
Hayward & Starlette Jean

GUIDED PRAYER FOCUS

THE FOUNDATION OF THE POWER CORD PRAYER JOURNAL

Let's think for a moment. Most appliances have power cords that connect them to the main electricity supply. In other words, the power cord is the way the appliance receives power. A marriage between a husband and a wife has a limited supply of power, but a marriage between a husband, a wife, and Jesus Christ dedicated to God has unlimited power! A powerful marriage is your love for God, your love for each other, and your love for others you influence. This type of marriage helps you to glorify God in every aspect of your marital relationship and to be a light to others for them to do the same.

As easy as this sounds, the following through of this as an intention doesn't happen without attacks from an enemy that opposes the standard God has set for marriage. "The thief cometh not, but for to steal, and to kill, and to destroy: I am come that they might have life, and that they might have it more abundantly." (John 10:10)

As the power cord is the way of power to an appliance, our relationship with Jesus Christ is the *way* we access the power for our marriages. He is the power source of our marriages. He is the one whom God ordained power for His glory. Contrary to what many believe, Christ is not Jesus' last name, but it represents the authority given to Him by God as the Anointed One, with the power to save souls and reconcile them to God. When we invite God as the primary source for our marriages, we have the ability to allow His power to flow through us in order to sustain the marriage, no matter the attacks that come against us, so that our marriages will glorify Him.

Prayer is how we communicate with God, and how to become one with Him through Jesus Christ. Many marriages often have prayer times: A married couple may pray in the morning, over meals, before bed, and/or in case an emergency arises. However, you and your spouse do not have 'married' times, but you have a married life. In that spirit, a prayer life is better for you than prayer times. While having prayer times as a married couple is okay, those times are more effective if they come from a prayer life. A married life of prayer creates and sustains oneness with God and your spouse.

Amos 3:3 says, "Can two walk together, except they be agreed?" In order to fulfill our purpose for marriage and maximize what we are able to do as a team, marriages must operate in a spirit of unity. Prayer is the place where we learn to submit and agree.

When a marriage operates in oneness, the marriage then becomes a mountain-moving marriage. Mountains represent what's hindering you, an obstacle, or a daring challenge. To properly move a mountain figuratively, you must first identify the mountain you are trying to move. Next, you must be intentional about moving that mountain and genuinely work to have the best marriage you can have.

Enjoy this 40-day journey of prayer as a couple. Always remember, we do have a real enemy that is against marriages, and that enemy is not your spouse. Today, with the choice to start this prayer journey, recommit to fighting in prayer together with and for your spouse. Pray for your marriage and for each other.

"A married prayer life" allows you to lead your marriage, seed your marriage, and feed your marriage because you have a need for your marriage.

Allow this prayer journal to empower you and your marriage. With the investment of prayer, look for a return of more love, more joy, and more peace from God. Believe for love to abound more and more in your marriage (Philippians 1:9).

THE SIGNIFICANCE
AND POWER OF 40 DAYS

In the Bible, the number forty represents a testing period, a time of fasting and consecration for great deliverance. At the end of forty days, many promises were fulfilled, and the grace for spiritual strength, maturity, and integrity was provided so that the recipient would be a good steward of those promises. A forty-day period was also the number that represented a cleansing and an opportunity to renew and refresh one's sense of believing and understanding.

Every encounter in the scriptures that had the command for a forty-day timeframe, resulted in victory. While the journey may not have been easy, it was worthwhile.

In Acts Chapter 7, Stephen gives the historical account when Moses was commanded to leave Egypt after 40 years. He then went and spent 40 years in the desert before God used him to lead the children of Israel out of slavery.

While Moses led the people out of physical bondage, they were still in emotional, mental, and spiritual bondage. Moses then spent 40 days and 40 nights seeking direction on how to lead such a large group of people in a way that would honor God and have integrity. Life after the 40 days and nights was not free from flaws or pain. However, the timeframe made room for God to truly see Moses' yearning for His direction and His blessings. Moses recognized he had to make a huge sacrifice because the calling was great, and he could not lead alone.

The children of Israel's journey to the promised land took 40 years, even though it should have only taken a few days. The delay wasn't because they didn't know which way to go, but because they were intimidated by the process necessary to access that promised land.

The 40 years in the wilderness was due to the decree of God for the whole generation to die in the wilderness so their children might possess the land. If they had only trusted and believed that the God who delivered them from Egypt, parted the Red Sea for them to walk on dry land, and used that same sea as a weapon to destroy their enemies, was able to empower them to possess the land. Instead, they considered their own strength and never considered the One who had already demonstrated His strength and love toward them.

Your marriage is a promised journey that will only result in good success and an overcoming victory when you depend on the God of your marriage more than the willpower of your flesh. Your marriage is not designed to flourish without Him. God has many promises to fulfill and wants your marriage to experience prosperity in every area of your lives, but He needs you to pursue and seek Him in prayer so you can rid yourselves of everything not needed in you. He does not want our marriages filled with compromise, discord, selfishness, opposition, lack of grace, bad speech, insecurities, and a disregard of our vows. NO! He wants us to enter a new promise, filled with agape love; the unconditional love of the Father for us.

During the 40 days of prayer as outlined here, married couples have an opportunity to refocus, and as a team, be empowered to overcome the lust of the flesh, temptations, chaos, insecurities, lack of motivation, pity, lack of passion, lack of two-way communication, and so much more. At the end of the 40-day prayer journey, the goal is for your marriage to be empowered and confident to use their most powerful weapon of all: prayer with authority.

PRAYER FOR MARRIAGES

Heavenly Father:

We are grateful for every couple that makes the decision to use this journal as a place to plan, grow, worship, and hear your intent for their marriages. We acknowledge that we have a real enemy who hates and is threatened by every power couple you have allowed to come together, but we declare we can do all things because you are the source of our strength. You have equipped us with every resource we need to overcome the attacks against marriages.

Your Word alone is filled with an abundance of promises we can declare to be the successful husbands and wives you intend for us to be. Help all couples to realize that we are only as great as the investments we sow into our marriage, and the greatest investment we will ever make is a consistent prayer life.

Lord, we believe that through this 40-day prayer journey, couples will pray together, and their marriages will be refreshed and restored in a new way.

Father, we pray that every husband and wife will develop a more intimate relationship with you that will lend itself to a more intimate relationship with each other. Father in Heaven, lift the broken, restore the joy, bring a refreshing, and show every couple we can always experience something new in you.

We stand on your Word that declares, "What therefore God hath joined together, let no man put asunder" Mark 10:9. We commit to taking this journey to fight united with and for our spouses, families, and communities in prayer.

In Jesus' name, Amen!

PRAYER FOCUS #1

PRAY FOR YOUR SPOUSE

The Unbreakable Cord of Marriage

The unbreakable cord of marriage is a threefold cord made up of a husband, a wife, and God, Himself. Successful marriages aren't unbreakable simply because couples say or think they can't be broken. Successful marriages are unbreakable because of the daily choices and actions to honor God, honor each other, and commit to the 'Fight of Faith' for a marriage. Their unbreakable confession is an expression of their union's commitment. When couples understand that the enemy's fight is against the union itself, and the marriage partners are on the same team, they will guard their hearts and allow Christ to protect their covenant.

Marriage is God's idea! When the world and the animal inhabitants were created, and man was formed, one could conclude Adam thought he was doing just fine with his animals. The Word of God states in Genesis 2:18(AMPC), "Now the Lord God said, It is not good (sufficient, satisfactory) that the man should be alone; I will make him a helper (suitable, adapted, complementary) for him."

God builds strong families based on His idea of marriage. Traditionally, marriage vows are exchanged at the altar. This symbolizes the consecration of marriages. When we said, "I do," access was granted to be an unbreakable power couple. A secret weapon lies within husbands and wives. This is the reason the enemy hates and agitates unions so much.

Satan and accompanying evil forces are threatened by couples that understand their ability to work together. His desire is to distract and destroy the unbreakable cord. Your spouse can do for you what no one else can. Your spouse is anointed to pray for you through some of the toughest and greatest seasons in your life.

Understand that God's vision for your marriage is to see Himself within it. When He looks at your marriage on earth, He's looking for a reflection of the way He loved, embraced, and gave His son for the Church. God cannot see Himself through something that is broken. He is not a breakable God. No matter what couples face they have the power to overcome and rise above the attacks and fiery darts (Ephesians 6:16) set out to destroy them, together, through Christ. `

To continue seeking Christ for the harmony of the marriage is essential. When elements of the marriage seem to be out of order, together in prayer with your spouse, continue to fight the good fight of faith, as I Timothy 6:12 tells us to. Be encouraged as you pray to have a marriage that will not be broken.

DAY 1

QUOTE OF THE DAY

"The unbreakable cord of marriage is a threefold cord made up of a husband, a wife, and God, Himself. Successful marriages are unbreakable because of the daily choices and actions to honor God, honor each other, and commit to the 'Fight of Faith' for a marriage."

THE POWER CORD

SCRIPTURE OF THE DAY

"And though one can overpower him who is alone, two can resist him. A cord of three strands is not quickly broken."

ECCLESIASTES 4:12

Reflection...

(Reflect on how the quote and scripture of the day can positively impact your marriage.)

My prayer focus today is...

Lord, I give you praise and thanksgiving for...

DAY 2

QUOTE OF THE DAY

"Marriage is God's idea. It is not designed to fail."
THE POWER CORD

SCRIPTURE OF THE DAY

"But from the beginning of the creation God made them male and female. For this cause shall a man leave his father and mother, and cleave to his wife; And they twain shall be one flesh: so then they are no more twain, but one flesh. What therefore God hath joined together, let no man put asunder."
MARK 10:6-9

Reflection...

(Reflect on how the quote and scripture of the day can positively impact your marriage.)

My prayer focus today is...

Lord, I give you praise and thanksgiving for...

DAY 3

QUOTE OF THE DAY

"Remember, you are anointed to pray for your spouse through some of the toughest and greatest seasons in their life. Be a safe place for your spouse to land."

THE POWER CORD

SCRIPTURE OF THE DAY

"Two are better than one; because they have a good reward for their labour. For if they fall, the one will lift up his fellow: but woe to him that is alone when he falleth; for he hath not another to help him up."

ECCLESIASTES 4:9-10

Reflection...

(Reflect on how the quote and scripture of the day can positively impact your marriage.)

My prayer focus today is...

Lord, I give you praise and thanksgiving for...

DAY 4

QUOTE OF THE DAY

"Let love drive the decisions you make in
marriage. When each spouse is loving
and serving the other, both spouses'
desires and needs will be met."

THE POWER CORD

SCRIPTURE OF THE DAY

*"For, brethren, ye have been called unto liberty; only use not
liberty for an occasion to the flesh, but by love serve one another."*

GALATIANS 5:13

Reflection...

(Reflect on how the quote and scripture of the day can positively impact your marriage.)

My prayer focus today is...

Lord, I give you praise and thanksgiving for...

PRAYER FOCUS #2

PRAY FOR HUMILITY IN YOUR MARRIAGE

Give Up—No More Power-Tripping

According to biblical principles, the design is for the husband to serve as head (Ephesians 5:23) of the wife and the wife to serve as help-meet (Genesis 2:18). Marriage is an institution in which both husband and wife should be able to benefit from one another. Marriage is not a dictatorship, but it is a covenant of valuing each other's roles, thoughts, and ideas, and lends itself to having a marriage where the husband is not trying to prove his manhood, and the wife is not trying to prove her independence. It is a marriage's interdependence that makes it powerful!

When we allow our roles or spiritual authority in marriage to get in the way of receiving help from one another, we open doors and create opportunities for our emotions to lead our decision-making. Valuing your spouse is essential as you continue to strive towards having and maintaining a healthy relationship. Each spouse must make room for the other's abilities, emotions, experiences, and talents when it comes to making decisions. Considering one another is one of the most amazing ways to honor each other in marriage.

Another term for power-tripping in marriage is self-centeredness. Marriage is not about who's in *charge*, but it is about fulfilling the *charge* of the union. The decision of both marital partners to submit to Christ's power will result in guaranteed fulfillment in the marriage. A lot of marriages are giving up on the wrong thing in their union. Instead of giving up *on* each other and giving up *on* the marriage, we should be giving up *for* each other and giving *up* for marriage. This is not a foreign thought, because when we decided to marry our spouses, we gave *up* our rights to singlehood.

In the scriptures, Christ not only gave *up* his life for us, but he gave us an example of what we should be doing for Him and our spouses. Galatians 2:20 says, "I am crucified with Christ: nevertheless, I live; yet not I, but Christ liveth in me: and the life which I now live in the flesh I live by the faith of the Son of God, who loved me, and gave Himself for me."

Giving up for our spouse isn't one-sided. A burger isn't done if we only cook it on one side. To be well-done, both sides must be cooked.

We don't want lopsided marriages. God doesn't control us; He leads and guides us to all truth. Be of good cheer as you pray that your marriage is filled with honor, and you choose to give *up* control, so that your greatest power will come from the spirit of humility in marriage.

DAY 5

QUOTE OF THE DAY

"Mutually honor each other's
role in your marriage."

THE POWER CORD

SCRIPTURE OF THE DAY

"Submitting yourselves one to another in the fear of God."

EPHESIANS 5:21

Reflection...

(Reflect on how the quote and scripture of the day can positively impact your marriage.)

My prayer focus today is...

Lord, I give you praise and thanksgiving for...

DAY 6

QUOTE OF THE DAY

"Marriage is not about who's in charge but submitting to the charge in your marriage and fulfilling the goals of the union."

THE POWER CORD

SCRIPTURE OF THE DAY

"But he giveth more grace. Wherefore he saith, God resisteth the proud, but giveth grace unto the humble. Submit yourselves therefore to God. Resist the devil, and he will flee from you."

JAMES 4:6-7

Reflection...

(Reflect on how the quote and scripture of the day can positively impact your marriage.)

My prayer focus today is...

Lord, I give you praise and thanksgiving for...

DAY 7

QUOTE OF THE DAY

"What goes on in a marriage is not about control;
allow your spouse to positively influence you."

THE POWER CORD

SCRIPTURE OF THE DAY

*"With all lowliness and meekness, with long-suffering,
forbearing one another in love; Endeavouring to keep
the unity of the Spirit in the bond of peace."*

EPHESIANS 4:2-3

Reflection...

(Reflect on how the quote and scripture of the day can positively impact your marriage.)

My prayer focus today is...

Lord, I give you praise and thanksgiving for...

DAY 8

QUOTE OF THE DAY

"Expect a marriage filled with honor,
balance and mutual submission
as you choose to give up control."

THE POWER CORD

SCRIPTURE OF THE DAY

"*I am crucified with Christ: nevertheless I live; yet not I, but Christ liveth in me: and the life which I now live in the flesh I live by the faith of the Son of God, who loved me, and gave himself for me.*"

GALATIANS 2:20

Reflection...

(Reflect on how the quote and scripture of the day can positively impact your marriage.)

My prayer focus today is...

Lord, I give you praise and thanksgiving for...

PRAYER FOCUS #3

PRAY FOR THE LEVELS OF INTIMACY IN YOUR MARRIAGE

Feed the Fire: The Truth About Intimacy

Intimacy comes from the Latin word, *intimare*, which means impress or make familiar, which comes from the Latin word, *"intimus,"* meaning *"inmost."* Many marriages fail when a spouse has the idea that intimacy is only sex. Intimacy is deeper than physical intimacy. Intimacy is the opportunity to connect with your spouse in ways you should not connect with anyone else. In marriage, intimacy is designed to allow each other access to share, explore, listen to, and be listened to while growing deeper together daily.

In order for physical intimacy to be enjoyable in the ways desired by both husband and wife in a marriage, all levels of intimacy must be invested in. Our spouses need to be impacted and touched by us spiritually, emotionally, intellectually, and physically.

In marriage, it is important yet challenging sometimes to have tough or uncomfortable conversations. An intimidation we may feel in intimacy can be overcome when couples face the giants in this area together. Marriage partners, remember that in the safety of prayer you have the power to face fears and walk in the authority of being more than conquerors (Romans 8:37).

Feed the fire and rekindle the intimacy of your marriage. A common saying tells us that what you don't feed will eventually starve. Couples, decide you will not starve the intimate moments of your marriages.

Investments must be made in order to stay connected in this most vulnerable area of our marriages. Couples, let's recognize that intimacy is so powerful it is the place where newness is conceived. When we embrace intimacy, we birth children, inventions, healthy emotions, and many positive, productive ideas. Many factors lie at the base of why intimacy is suffocated in marriage. These reasons include ill health, insecurity, fatigue, work worries, work relationships, family relationships and much more.

Make space for a satisfying and passionate intimate marriage; plan for sex, write "just because" love letters, pray together, read as a family, touch each other affectionately, be honest, renew your vows often, and workout together. These are just a few ideas. As you seek God together you will experience so many more. Allow Him to stir the intimacy in your marriage in order to resist staleness and produce abundant joy. New life is produced from true intimacy in marriage.

DAY 9

QUOTE OF THE DAY

"The physical fire of your marriage will
not be strong if you aren't feeding the
inward fire of your relationship."

THE POWER CORD

SCRIPTURE OF THE DAY

*"Let thy fountain be blessed: and rejoice with the wife of thy youth.
Let her be as the loving hind and pleasant roe; let her breasts
satisfy thee at all times; and be thou ravish always with her love."*

PROVERBS 5:18-19

Reflection...

(Reflect on how the quote and scripture of the day can positively impact your marriage.)

My prayer focus today is...

Lord, I give you praise and thanksgiving for...

DAY 10

QUOTE OF THE DAY

"Plan for intimacy in your marriage."
THE POWER CORD

SCRIPTURE OF THE DAY

*"Marriage is honourable in all, and the bed undefiled:
but whoremongers and adulterers God will judge."*
HEBREWS 13:4

Reflection...

(Reflect on how the quote and scripture of the day can positively impact your marriage.)

My prayer focus today is...

Lord, I give you praise and thanksgiving for...

DAY 11

QUOTE OF THE DAY

"Think of ways to honor
intimacy in your marriage."

THE POWER CORD

SCRIPTURE OF THE DAY

"Let the husband render unto the wife due benevolence: and likewise also the wife unto the husband. The wife hath not power of her own body, but the husband: and likewise also the husband hath not power of his own body, but the wife."

1 CORINTHIANS 7:3-4

Reflection...

(Reflect on how the quote and scripture of the day can positively impact your marriage.)

My prayer focus today is...

Lord, I give you praise and thanksgiving for...

DAY 12

QUOTE OF THE DAY

"When small foxes come to destroy your intimacy, fan the flame in your marriage. Keep the firing burning on purpose."

THE POWER CORD

SCRIPTURE OF THE DAY

"Come, my beloved, let us go forth into the field; let us lodge in the villages. Let us get up early to the vineyards; let us see if the vine flourish, whether the tender grape appear, and the pomegranates bud forth: there will I give thee my loves."

SONG OF SOLOMON 7:11-12

Reflection...

(Reflect on how the quote and scripture of the day can positively impact your marriage.)

My prayer focus today is...

Lord, I give you praise and thanksgiving for...

PRAYER FOCUS #4

PRAY FOR UNITY IN YOUR MARRIAGE

Avoid the Power Struggle:
You Are Better Together

"As iron sharpens iron, so one man sharpens [and influences] another [through discussion]." Proverbs 27:17. Iron sharpening in marriage is designed to strengthen and build marriages. The iron sharpening in marriage is never meant to cut, tear down, or destroy your spouse. Sharpening refines the purpose of marriage and purifies the roles of spouses. The key to this purpose alignment is submission.

The world categorizes submission as a sign of weakness and inferiority. However, submission in Kingdom of God marriages is one of the greatest strengths of a successful marriage. Submission works as a yielding in marriage, just as a yield sign works on roadways. It allows for a better flow of two objects.

In the marriage, the two people generally want to go in the same direction, but without submission or yielding, a crash is inevitable.

When couples are unified and intentionally work together, with Christ at the center, the marriage is purpose-driven and not person-driven. Submitting is a mutual expectation for both husband and wife (Ephesians 5:21) with separate directives for the wife to submit to the husband (Ephesians 5:22,24), and the husband to submit to God for the marriage (Ephesians 5:25).

We should always be encouraged to avoid unhealthy competition in marriage. Couples, be charged and encouraged to believe you are unstoppable when you master the "united we stand" mentality in the union.

Most confrontations and disagreements are avoidable in marriage when a husband and wife commit to honoring each other's voice in marriage. Honoring one another's voice makes your marriage beautiful, because you are showing your spouse you respect what they say, think, or believe.

When couples operate together, they begin to see ideas unfold and improve as they listen to one another. When you listen to your spouse, honor your spouse's voice, and work together in marriage, this can bring healing, physical health and spiritual unity in marriage.

Marriage is about foregoing selfish ways and serving the one, to whom you have made a commitment. Being selfless is not about losing your identity, it simply means you make a decision to yield, saying "I prefer your good to mine." The beauty of both spouses making a decision to deny themselves and serve the other means everyone's needs will be met.

When you adopt a unified mentality in marriage, you will shut down the distractions and temptations of challenging each other's authority, and you leave no room for a marital power struggle. Pray for a spirit of unity in your marriage and forever strive to be intentional about operating in oneness.

DAY 13

QUOTE OF THE DAY

"Avoid unhealthy competition in your marriage."
THE POWER CORD

SCRIPTURE OF THE DAY

"Let nothing be done through strife or vainglory; but in lowliness of mind let each esteem other better than themselves. Look not every man on his own things, but every man also on the things of others."

PHILIPPIANS 2:3-4

Reflection...

(Reflect on how the quote and scripture of the day can positively impact your marriage.)

My prayer focus today is...

Lord, I give you praise and thanksgiving for...

DAY 14

QUOTE OF THE DAY

"It is important to honor the voice of your spouse. Honoring one another's voices makes your marriage beautiful, because you are showing your spouse you respect what they say, think, or believe."

THE POWER CORD

SCRIPTURE OF THE DAY

"And let us consider one another to provoke unto love and to good works: Not forsaking the assembling of ourselves together, as the manner of some is; but exhorting one another: and so much the more, as ye see the day approaching."

HEBREWS 10:24-25

Reflection...

(Reflect on how the quote and scripture of the day can positively impact your marriage.)

My prayer focus today is...

Lord, I give you praise and thanksgiving for...

DAY 15

QUOTE OF THE DAY

"As a couple we haven't mastered how to do marriage without fault, so we should be striving to grow, work together, and be the best we can be daily, just as we should be doing regarding our relationship with God."

THE POWER CORD

SCRIPTURE OF THE DAY

"Now I beseech you, brethren by the name of our Lord Jesus Christ, that ye all speak the same thing, and that there be no divisions among you; but that ye be perfectly joined together in the same mind and in the same judgement."

1 CORINTHIANS 1:10

Reflection...

(Reflect on how the quote and scripture of the day can positively impact your marriage.)

My prayer focus today is...

Lord, I give you praise and thanksgiving for...

DAY 16

QUOTE OF THE DAY

"When you adopt a unified mentality in marriage, you will shut down the distractions and temptations of challenging each other's authority."

THE POWER CORD

SCRIPTURE OF THE DAY

"Fulfill ye my joy, that ye be likeminded, having the same love, being of one accord, of one mind."

PHILLIPIANS 2:2

Reflection...

(Reflect on how the quote and scripture of the day can positively impact your marriage.)

My prayer focus today is...

Lord, I give you praise and thanksgiving for...

PRAYER FOCUS #5

PRAY FOR ORDER IN YOUR MARRIAGE

Personal Life vs. Professional Life

Never underestimate the power of prayer in your personal life because prayer in this area is extremely important. We have heard the saying for so long, "you are what you eat." Let's go a step further, look at what happens when you don't eat for an extended period. You can only go on empty for so long. Eventually without the proper nourishment, life comes to an end.

When you are invested in feeling like, "I can't spend quality time with my spouse because I have to work countless hours to provide for my spouse," the solution is difficult to envision. You are not just a professional who clocks in and out of a job. You are a professional who must nourish your personal life.

But you must start by dismissing the idea that your marriage will only survive because of material things. In fact, you and your spouse must invest in your personal lives because your personal lives are more important than your professional lives. You will be a better professional once you prioritize your marriage.

Winning the fight between your personal life and your professional life doesn't result from your fists, but rather by winning a fight with your mindset. If you will turn to the Lord to order your marriage steps, the resolution will fall into place. You cannot balance your personal life and your professional life because the two are not equals.

All too often we become (needlessly) overwhelmed and busy with the affairs of everyday life. With the same level of intentionality, we have about our day–to-day schedules, we must prioritize and be intentional about praying with and for our spouses. "When the Lord is esteemed above all things and our ways as people, it's His pleasure to give you the desires of your heart (Psalm 37). Have the mentality in your marriage that "we" will WIN; "we" are champions, and with the guidance of the Lord, He will order "our" steps.

DAY 17

QUOTE OF THE DAY

"Winning the fight between your personal life and your professional life doesn't result from your fists, but rather by winning a fight with your mindset."

THE POWER CORD

SCRIPTURE OF THE DAY

"Let all things be done decently and in order."

1 CORINTHIANS 14:40

Reflection...

(Reflect on how the quote and scripture of the day can positively impact your marriage.)

My prayer focus today is...

Lord, I give you praise and thanksgiving for...

DAY 18

QUOTE OF THE DAY

"Don't stop being faithful to your marriage simply because you may not see the same level of faithfulness from your spouse. Continue to pray, press on, and pursue."

THE POWER CORD

SCRIPTURE OF THE DAY

"And let us not be weary in well doing: for in due season we shall reap, if we faint not."

GALATIANS 6:9

Reflection...

(Reflect on how the quote and scripture of the day can positively impact your marriage.)

My prayer focus today is...

Lord, I give you praise and thanksgiving for...

DAY 19

QUOTE OF THE DAY

"You are not just a professional who clocks
in and out of a job. You are a professional
who must nourish your personal life."

THE POWER CORD

SCRIPTURE OF THE DAY

*"Delight thyself also in the Lord: and he shall
give thee the desires of thine heart."*

PSALM 37:4

Reflection...

(Reflect on how the quote and scripture of the day can positively impact your marriage.)

My prayer focus today is...

Lord, I give you praise and thanksgiving for...

DAY 20

QUOTE OF THE DAY

"May your marriage mirror the consistency, patience, and love that Christ has for His Church."

THE POWER CORD

SCRIPTURE OF THE DAY

"That there should be no schism in the body; but that the members should have the same care one for another."

1 CORINTHIANS 12:25

Reflection...

(Reflect on how the quote and scripture of the day can positively impact your marriage.)

My prayer focus today is...

Lord, I give you praise and thanksgiving for...

PRAYER FOCUS #6

PRAY FOR POSITIVE COMMUNICATION IN YOUR MARRIAGE

What Communication Service Are You Providing?

Activate the Power of Speaking Life

James 3:3-6 says, "Now if we put bits into the horses' mouths to make them obey us, we guide their whole body as well. And look at the ships. Even though they are so large and are driven by strong winds, they are still directed by a very small rudder wherever the impulse of the helmsman determines. In the same sense, the tongue is a small part of the body, and yet it boasts of great things. See [by comparison] how great a forest is set on fire by a small spark! And the tongue is [in a sense] a fire, the *very* world of injustice *and* unrighteousness; the tongue is set among our members as that which contaminates the entire body and sets on fire the course of our life [the cycle of man's existence] and is itself set on fire by hell."

From "I do" to "we're through," the tongue can be used to start or end a marriage. Every moment of the day, we have a choice to use our words to strengthen or weaken our marriages. If one statement at the altar started a life of holy matrimony, how much more can one statement of anger, sarcasm, or cynicism start a life of utter misery and resentment. The power of Christ in our marriage is the power that gives us the ability to allow Him, the Anointed One, to help us control our tongues.

Without Christ in us serving as the helmsman of our conversation, we are sometimes a phrase away from causing shipwrecks in our marriage. However, with Christ in us, we are often a phrase away from the greatest miracle in our marriage. While the tongue is often the center of attention for monumental moments in marriage, it is even more significant in the mundane moments, such as day-to-day communication. Don't take for granted the power of the tongue in your everyday language with your spouse. Positive communication in marriage is essential to building and maintaining a healthy relationship. It is not absent from conflict, but it does allow you to stay focused on resolution instead of revenge in the conflict.

Picture going to your favorite restaurant and the server comes to take your order. Instead of giving you what you ask, the server decides it is a better idea for you to try their favorite dish. In this case, your best interest was not on the mind of the one serving you. In the same vein, our positive communication should always have the best interest of our spouse in mind.

One of the most effective ways to promote healthy communication in our marriages is to serve the tone that works for the one being served. The heart of any server should be to make sure the recipient is taken care of. In marriage, communication will not always be pleasant to hear, but positive communication in marriage is about taking care of your spouse during the exchange. Ask yourself, "What communication am I serving?' Pray for a marriage filled with positive communication and allow God to activate the power of speaking life.

DAY 21

QUOTE OF THE DAY

"Choose and use the language that produces
the life God desires for your marriage."

THE POWER CORD

SCRIPTURE OF THE DAY

*"Pleasant words are as a honeycomb, sweet
to the soul and health to the bones."*

PROVERBS 16:24

Reflection...

(Reflect on how the quote and scripture of the day can positively impact your marriage.)

My prayer focus today is...

Lord, I give you praise and thanksgiving for...

DAY 22

QUOTE OF THE DAY

"Nature began with a word. You have the
same ability to speak what you want to
see in your marriage and let it be!"

THE POWER CORD

SCRIPTURE OF THE DAY

*"Death and life are in the power of the tongue: and they
that love it shall eat the fruit thereof. Whoso findeth a wife
findeth a good thing, and obtaineth favour of the Lord."*

PROVERBS 18:21-22

Reflection...

(Reflect on how the quote and scripture of the day can positively impact your marriage.)

My prayer focus today is...

Lord, I give you praise and thanksgiving for...

DAY 23

QUOTE OF THE DAY

"Be intentional about building up your spouse with your words. When you build up your spouse and your spouse is building you up, the marriage is being built."

THE POWER CORD

SCRIPTURE OF THE DAY

"Set a watch, O Lord, before my mouth; keep the door of my lips."

PSALM 141:3

Reflection...

(Reflect on how the quote and scripture of the day can positively impact your marriage.)

My prayer focus today is...

Lord, I give you praise and thanksgiving for...

DAY 24

QUOTE OF THE DAY

"Communication in your marriage is
your lifeline in a time of crisis."

THE POWER CORD

SCRIPTURE OF THE DAY

*"Let your speech be always with grace, seasoned with salt,
that you may know how ye ought to answer every man."*

COLOSSIANS 4:6

Reflection...

(Reflect on how the quote and scripture of the day can positively impact your marriage.)

My prayer focus today is...

Lord, I give you praise and thanksgiving for...

PRAYER FOCUS #7

PRAY FOR JOY IN YOUR MARRIAGE

Love, Laugh, and Rejoice Together

One word that can irrevocably change the course of your marriage is joy. Joy is different from happiness. While happiness is rooted in how you feel, joy is a delight rooted in what you know. Joy can be experienced with or without happiness. Some people may think, you can't be happy all the time. The truth is sometimes you simply won't be happy. But also at times, happiness isn't the emotion needed in your marriage to accomplish a task. There are times you need a spirit of anger—a type of anger that is blameless and free of sin—to attack or come against something that could be trying to destroy your marriage. Sometimes, your marriage requires reasoning and deep thought.

Sometimes, you face challenges that do not necessarily place you against your spouse, but you face difficulties together, especially during times of sorrow and sadness. We aren't saying to be happy in times of sadness, but we are saying we always have time for JOY!

Happiness has a lot to do with what happens externally such as when people do something for you, or you may have seen something that makes you happy. However, joy is a power beyond reason that comes from within. You can maintain a joy that will not allow what your spouse does or does not do for you to dictate how you respond.

Joy can be extremely powerful in your marriage. Just as the focus of the Power Cord is to be intentional about making sure Christ is the center of your marriage, be encouraged in knowing that when

Christ came to the earth, this was joy coming to the world. The same can be true for your marriage: joy to your marriage for the Lord has come!

You or your spouse may have spoken negatively and/or done something in your marriage that was an unwise choice, but the beautiful thing is, according to God's holy word, *the joy of the Lord is your strength.* (Nehemiah 8:10.) You will want to have a genuine mentality in your marriage that the joy inside of you is greater than the thing that tried to come against you.

Joy is not a seasonal emotion. We don't only look to have joy in our marriage during the holidays. Joy can be experienced throughout your marriage, throughout the year. Experiencing this joy goes deep. It requires faith-filled conversation, hopeful reflections, and loving actions with much prayer and studying the word of God!

When there is no joy inside of a marriage, the couple often find themselves just, "going through the motion." Think about the things that used to bring your spouse joy that you may not do anymore. What can be done differently in your marriage or what can be done the same, but in a different way that will inspire this joy?

During this prayer focus, seek the Lord concerning ways you and your spouse can put a little more effort into restoring or maintaining the joy in your marriage. Don't allow situational happiness to compete with your marital joy. With Christ, joy can thrive every day in your marriage. Let joy be your marriage story. If Christ came for us to have joy, take it! Joy to the world and joy to your marriage!

DAY 25

QUOTE OF THE DAY

"Joy in marriage can remain even when happiness in marriage is constrained."

THE POWER CORD

SCRIPTURE OF THE DAY

"Rejoice in the Lord always: and again I say, Rejoice."

PHILIPPIANS 4:4

Reflection...

(Reflect on how the quote and scripture of the day can positively impact your marriage.)

My prayer focus today is...

Lord, I give you praise and thanksgiving for...

DAY 26

QUOTE OF THE DAY

"Joy adds value *to* your marriage, because it allows you to constantly see the value *in* your marriage."

THE POWER CORD

SCRIPTURE OF THE DAY

"Let the word of Christ dwell in you richly in all wisdom; teaching and admonishing one another in psalms and hymns and spiritual songs, singing with grace in your hearts to the Lord. And whatsoever ye do in word or deed, do all in the name of the Lord Jesus, giving thanks to God and the Father by him."

COLOSSIANS 3:16-17

Reflection...

(Reflect on how the quote and scripture of the day can positively impact your marriage.)

My prayer focus today is...

Lord, I give you praise and thanksgiving for...

DAY 27

QUOTE OF THE DAY

"Don't hold back the joy in your marriage.
Let it flow!"

THE POWER CORD

SCRIPTURE OF THE DAY

*"A merry heart maketh a cheerful countenance: but
by sorrow of the heart the spirit is broken."*

PROVERBS 15:13

Reflection...

(Reflect on how the quote and scripture of the day can positively impact your marriage.)

My prayer focus today is...

Lord, I give you praise and thanksgiving for...

DAY 28

QUOTE OF THE DAY

"Joy in marriage is a reward from God
that is available to you at all times."

THE POWER CORD

SCRIPTURE OF THE DAY

*"Live joyfully with the wife whom thou lovest all the days
of the life of thy vanity, which he hath given thee under the
sun, all the days of thy vanity: for that is thy portion in this
life, and in thy labour which thou takest under the sun."*

ECCLESIASTES 9:9

Reflection...

(Reflect on how the quote and scripture of the day can positively impact your marriage.)

My prayer focus today is...

Lord, I give you praise and thanksgiving for...

PRAYER FOCUS #8

PRAY TO LOVE YOUR SPOUSE UNCONDITIONALLY

Hold No Grudges. Give Your Spouse Space for Grace

Oftentimes, from the world's culture we learn how to hold onto something someone has done to or against us. We say, "I can forgive, but I won't forget." This culture has set for us an identity of marriage that often subscribes to this thought. However, married couples must understand that the world's culture can't teach us about marriage, because it isn't the designer of marriage. Marriage isn't supposed to be viewed through the eyes of television, Hollywood, and/or fairy tales. Our marriages are intended to operate the way God sent Jesus to love and forgive the church.

In marriage, we must realize that at some point one or both partners will do or say something they didn't mean. Don't allow lack of grace to make you forget that before you loved your spouse, you liked your spouse. Before you became husband and wife, you were good friends. The goal is to not allow grudges to choke the life out of your friendship and marriage.

According to the Oxford Dictionary, grudges are feelings of anger or dislike toward somebody because of something bad they have done to you in the past. This is a form of unforgiveness. No doubt about it, these feelings hurt, but the toughest thing about a grudge comes when we decide to let it go.

Grudges impact your soul and the soul of your spouse. If you're a very soulful person, always living from your feelings and emotions, or always guarded and on the defense, the grudge can impact everything in your relationships. Grudges have the potential to make you overanalyze each word and deed. They can stay on your mind, plaguing you until you have absolutely no peace. They can constantly attack your emotions because you're in this stance of offense. While you may be reacting to something that was done to you (or so you feel), the grudge that you hold eventually becomes something that you are doing to yourself. Holding grudges restricts you and your spouse by robbing you of precious moments and memories. You've both invested too much into your marriage to allow a grudge to take it all away.

The same forgiveness that we want from God, we have to be willing to give to someone else, especially your spouse. The same level of grace we want from God, let's give to our partner in marriage.

When grudges occur, we usually have no plan for how we, as a couple, will diffuse the situation. We must make a plan or decision to forgive and let go of the grudges we're holding onto, then the frustrations and arguing will leave also. Pray to love your spouse unconditionally and for grace in your marriage; decide to forgive, move forward, and heal together. Yearn to live in a graceful marriage and enjoy life without the weight of grudges.

DAY 29

QUOTE OF THE DAY

"Mainstream media can't teach you about marriage because it didn't create marriage. Only God who instituted marriage and those who live out His idea of marriage can instruct, direct, and empower you to have a successful marriage. Stay connected to the Creator."

THE POWER CORD

SCRIPTURE OF THE DAY

"Wherefore, my beloved brethren, let every man be swift to hear, slow to speak, slow to wrath: For the wrath of man worketh not the righteousness of God."

JAMES 1:19-20

Reflection...

(Reflect on how the quote and scripture of the day can positively impact your marriage.)

My prayer focus today is...

Lord, I give you praise and thanksgiving for...

DAY 30

QUOTE OF THE DAY

"Allow each other the opportunity in marriage to learn without penalty."

THE POWER CORD

SCRIPTURE OF THE DAY

"And be ye kind one to another, tenderhearted, forgiving one another, even as God for Christ's sake hath forgiven you."

EPHESIANS 4: 32

Reflection...

(Reflect on how the quote and scripture of the day can positively impact your marriage.)

My prayer focus today is...

Lord, I give you praise and thanksgiving for...

DAY 31

QUOTE OF THE DAY

"The best time to make a plan for how to get out of the place of "grudgement," is when there are no grudges, we are feeling no frustrations, and we are not arguing."

THE POWER CORD

SCRIPTURE OF THE DAY

"And he said unto me, My grace is sufficient for thee: for my strength is made perfect in weakness. Most gladly therefore will I rather glory in my infirmities, that the power of Christ may rest upon me."

2 CORINTHIANS 12:9

Reflection...

(Reflect on how the quote and scripture of the day can positively impact your marriage.)

My prayer focus today is...

Lord, I give you praise and thanksgiving for...

DAY 32

QUOTE OF THE DAY

"No weapon formed against your marriage shall prosper. Fight with and for each other and not against each other."

THE POWER CORD

SCRIPTURE OF THE DAY

"Therefore all things whatsoever ye would that men should do to you, do ye even so to them: for this is the law and the prophets."

MATTHEW 7:12

Reflection...

(Reflect on how the quote and scripture of the day can positively impact your marriage.)

My prayer focus today is...

Lord, I give you praise and thanksgiving for...

PRAYER FOCUS #9

PRAY FOR A REFRESHING IN YOUR MARRIAGE

Have No More Staleness in Marriage

Often, consistency and familiarity produce drudgery and a monotony that allows a marriage to plateau or become stale. However, consistency and familiarity, when appropriately perceived, can become a building block and give way to a renewal and refreshing in your marriage.

Another factor that produces staleness is holding onto old ways in marriage that were good for where you once were but are no longer effective for where you are presently. For example, in the beginning of your marriage, you may have had a goal of saving $10 a month, because that was what you could afford in your employment status then. However, years later, your status has changed, and you may be able to save more. In marriage, your rationale for doing things should not be based on "that's the way we've always done it" but should be guided by cooperating with the Holy Spirit and God's plan for your life.

Communicating with God in prayer, should not take a backseat to the things of old, because you could miss the new things happening in your marriage. Consider how updates are being made on a computer or website. The only way to know if new information has been added is to refresh the site. Don't be afraid to leave the old because it's comfortable and fear the new because it is unknown. The new thing God wants to do in your marriage will produce new life.

Do not [earnestly] remember the former things; neither consider the things of old. Behold, I am doing a new thing! Now it springs forth; do you not perceive and know it and will you not give heed to it? I will even make a way in the wilderness and rivers in the desert. Isaiah 43:18-19.

God wants to give your marriage a refreshing. Embrace the new thing He wants to do in you. Pray for it!

DAY 33

QUOTE OF THE DAY

"Your first date wasn't sufficient to sustain the marriage. Keep pursuing one another."

THE POWER CORD

SCRIPTURE OF THE DAY

"The soul of the sluggard desireth, and hath nothing: but the soul of the diligent shall be made fat."

PROVERBS 13:4

Reflection...

(Reflect on how the quote and scripture of the day can positively impact your marriage.)

My prayer focus today is...

Lord, I give you praise and thanksgiving for...

DAY 34

QUOTE OF THE DAY

"Marriage motives: Whenever we invest in our marriage, we will see inner development with outer benefits."

THE POWER CORD

SCRIPTURE OF THE DAY

"But they that wait upon the Lord shall renew their strength; they shall mount up with wings as eagles; they shall run, and not be weary; and they shall walk, and not faint."

ISAIAH 40:31

Reflection...

(Reflect on how the quote and scripture of the day can positively impact your marriage.)

My prayer focus today is...

Lord, I give you praise and thanksgiving for...

DAY 35

QUOTE OF THE DAY

"Keep your hearts close to God, as
He keeps your hearts pure for marriage."
THE POWER CORD

SCRIPTURE OF THE DAY

*"This people draweth nigh unto me with their mouth, and
honoureth me with their lips; but their heart is far from me."*
MATTHEW 15:8

Reflection...

(Reflect on how the quote and scripture of the day can positively impact your marriage.)

My prayer focus today is...

Lord, I give you praise and thanksgiving for...

DAY 36

QUOTE OF THE DAY

"Work your marriage. Make a plan for how you will not allow your marriage to be stagnant."

THE POWER CORD

SCRIPTURE OF THE DAY

"Commit thy way unto the Lord;
trust also in him; and he shall bring it to pass."

PSALM 37:5

Reflection...

(Reflect on how the quote and scripture of the day can positively impact your marriage.)

My prayer focus today is...

Lord, I give you praise and thanksgiving for...

PRAYER FOCUS #10

PRAY FOR THE MISSION OF YOUR MARRIAGE

The Key to a Great Marriage

Those who enjoy great marriages in the Kingdom of God are zealous about serving one another, serving in their church, and serving their community. Healthy marriages produce healthy families, which lead to healthy communities. Jesus said, "But He that is greatest among you shall be your servant" (Matthew 23:11).

The greatest servant we know is Jesus. He was passionate about serving people. Because He is the Word made flesh (John 1:14), He didn't just talk the talk, but He became the Word of God, who walked the walk. The Word that came from God produced Jesus, who took on the form of a servant. (Philippians 2:7)

As Christians, we should be like Christ in the world. Since our marriages represent Christ and the church, we must be in service to each other, in our relationships as couples, before we can be of great service to others. The way we serve each other as spouses will produce the integrity and substance needed to serve others.

Service to each other should not be an event, but it should be a way of life and as ordinary to our marriages as breathing is to our beings. While monumental moments are great and require faith and focus, the ordinary moments in our marriages are what help to develop the purity and greatness of our love for each other. This love is honed in service.

Your marriage is a ministry that allows God to love others through you.

You don't have to be deep or have eloquence of speech to serve, but your service to your spouse requires faith in God, fervent love for your spouse, and a strong desire to see God's purpose for your spouse fulfilled. All this can be manifested through your energy, time, and effort that supports your spouse in a way which enhances and advances the mission of your marriage.

While it is easy to sit and be critical of the weaknesses of your spouse and of others, you can alternately be intentional and celebrate their strengths. By doing this you build on the positives while making the strengthening of weaknesses a faith project for both of you. As this approach within your marriage becomes the norm, your mission to serve others will produce a light that can inspire other marriages, while uplifting the people of your church and community. Glorify God in your marriage by loving each other the way Christ loved us and the way the church should love Him.

DAY 37

QUOTE OF THE DAY

"Seek rather to serve more in your marriage, than to seek to always gain something from your marriage."

THE POWER CORD

SCRIPTURE OF THE DAY

"Above all things have fervent charity among yourselves: for charity shall cover the multitude of sins."

1 PETER 4:8

Reflection...

(Reflect on how the quote and scripture of the day can positively impact your marriage.)

My prayer focus today is...

Lord, I give you praise and thanksgiving for...

DAY 38

QUOTE OF THE DAY

"Service to each other should not be an event, but it should be a way of life and as ordinary to our marriages as breathing is to our beings."

THE POWER CORD

SCRIPTURE OF THE DAY

"Charity suffereth long, and is kind; charity envieth not; charity vaunteth not itself, is not puffed up, Doth not behave itself unseemly, seeketh not her own, is not easily provoked, thinketh no evil; Rejoiceth not in iniquity, but rejoiceth in the truth; Beareth all things, believeth all things, hopeth all things, endureth all things."

1 CORINTHIANS 13:4-7

Reflection...

(Reflect on how the quote and scripture of the day can positively impact your marriage.)

My prayer focus today is...

Lord, I give you praise and thanksgiving for...

DAY 39

QUOTE OF THE DAY

"Remember, your marriage was blessed on the
altar. Don't forsake the covering by God that
was granted when you said, ``I will, and I do."

THE POWER CORD

SCRIPTURE OF THE DAY

"*For I know the thoughts that I think toward you, saith the Lord,
thoughts of peace, and not of evil, to give you an expected end.*"

JEREMIAH 29:11

Reflection...

(Reflect on how the quote and scripture of the day can positively impact your marriage.)

My prayer focus today is...

Lord, I give you praise and thanksgiving for...

DAY 40

QUOTE OF THE DAY

"Keep praying God's will for your marriage,
as you live God's will for your marriage."

THE POWER CORD

SCRIPTURE OF THE DAY

*"And this is the confidence that we have in him, that,
if we ask anything according to his will, he heareth us."*

1 JOHN 5:14

Reflection...

(Reflect on how the quote and scripture of the day can positively impact your marriage.)

My prayer focus today is...

Lord, I give you praise and thanksgiving for...

THANK YOU, POWER CORD COUPLES
(The end of our 40-day prayer journey)

We are grateful to God that you intentionally spent 40 days of prayer, investing time with God in your marriage for your marriage! We are believing God for you as you continue to sound the alarm and maintain being a praying wife and/or praying husband in your marriage.

It is our sincere prayer that you will not stop pursuing the Lord in the next steps and ways to enhance your marriage. Keep striving to be who Christ is for the church and who the church should be toward Christ.

We hope this prayer journal did exactly what it has been designed to do; bring joy, peace, understanding, and a deeper level of spiritual intimacy in your marriage.

Speak these marriage affirmations as you go and grow in LOVE:

My marriage will thrive as we remain
connected to God, the ultimate power source!
My marriage is not easily broken!
My marriage is a beautiful sight in the presence of God!
My marriage is a safe place!
My marriage is worth the sacrifice!
My spouse is a praying spouse!
My spouse is more than enough!

Thank you for taking this prayer journey with us.

Forever in our thoughts and prayers,
Hayward and Starlette Jean, The Power Cord

CERTIFICATE OF COMPLETION

This certificate is presented to

for successful completion of investing
40-days of prayer in marriage.

Continue to speak life in your marriage,
speak life to your marriage,
and speak life over your marriage!

Let's Connect!

Hayward and Starlette Jean

h a y w a r d j e a n . c o m

 @thepowercordmarriage

 @thepowercordmarriage

 thepowercordmarriage@gmail.com